Angels All
Around Me

Other Books
by Sarah Hornsby

At the Name of Jesus
Who I Am in Jesus
The Fruit of the Spirit
Standing Firm in Jesus
Jesus, Be in Me
Getting to Know Jesus from A to Z
Jesus, Be in My Christmas
Nicaragüense
Love Is . . .

Angels All Around Me

Angels in the Bible: What They Are Like, What They Have to Do with Me and You

Sarah Hornsby

Chosen Books

A Division of Baker Book House Co
Grand Rapids, Michigan 49516

© 1995 by Sarah Hornsby

Published by Chosen Books
a division of Baker Book House Company
P.O. Box 6287, Grand Rapids, Michigan 49516-6287

Printed in the United States of America

ISBN 0-8007-9225-4

To our guardian angels

Contents

Angels Are Created, Ministering Spirits   10

Angels Live Forever   12

Angels Are Majestic Beings   14

Angels Are Warriors   16

Angels Are Organized in Military Ranks   18

Angels Appear in Human Form   20

Angels Protect and Punish   22

Angels Connect Earth and Heaven to Strengthen
   God's People   24

Angels Do Miracles   26

Angels Are Usually Invisible   28

Angels Are Powerful   30

Angels Are Chosen by God for Special Missions   32

Angels Stand by God's People in Danger   34

Angels Provide   36

Angels Guard   38

Angels Are Wise   40

Angels Are God's Messengers   42

Angels Obey God's Will   44
Angels Announce Salvation   46
Angels Sing Praises to God   48
Angels Warn   50
Angels Help in Healing   52
Angels Comfort   54
Angels Are Joyful   56
Angels Strengthen   58
Angels Are Radiant   60
Angels Proclaim Jesus' Resurrection   62
Angels Ask Penetrating Questions   64
Angels Bring Judgment   66
Angels Carry Believers to God in Death   68
Angels Bring Peace   70
Angels Stand with Jesus' Followers   72
Angels Deliver   74
Angels Direct the Activities of God's People   76
Angels Witness   78
Angels Encourage   80
Angels Are Holy   82
Angels Are Harvesters   84
Angels Reveal What Is Real   86
Angels Are Guardians   88
Angel Stories   90

. . . Even when we are alone we are never alone, for we are joining the jubilee chant of angels and archangels and living creatures about which we can only guess. . . . In God's time and in God's way we are led irresistibly into the adoration of him who is eternal, immortal, invisible, the only wise God (1 Tim. 1:17). Richard Baxter urges us: "Be much in that angelic work of praise. As the most heavenly Spirits will have the most heavenly employment, so the more heavenly the employment the more it will make the spirit heavenly."

Richard J. Foster, Prayer

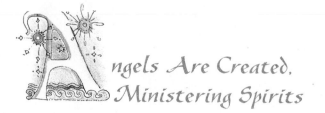

ngels Are Created, Ministering Spirits

Jesus created all things in heaven and on earth, visible and invisible. All thrones, powers [angels], rulers and authorities have been created by Him and for Him.

Colossians 1:16, author's paraphrase

Even before the earth and any people were created, God, with Jesus and the Holy Spirit, made beautiful, good beings we call angels. They live to serve God and praise Him, not to be praised. The Bible teaches us many things about them.

God also created you and me. Let's join the angels in praising Him for how wonderfully we are made!

Praise the LORD.
Praise the LORD from the heavens,
Praise him in the heights above.
Praise him, all his angels,
Praise him, all his heavenly hosts. . . .
Let them praise the name of the LORD,
For he commanded and they were created.
Psalm 148:1–2, 5

11

Angels Live Forever

"Those who are considered worthy of taking part in . . . the resurrection from the dead will neither marry nor be given in marriage, and they can no longer die; for they are like the angels."
Luke 20:35–36

All human beings will die. I will die and so will you. But that is just our physical bodies. Our spirits, when they are joined with Jesus, will live forever. Then we can see for ourselves all the wonders of God and what He has done through the angels.

When Jesus' beloved disciple, John, was imprisoned on Patmos Island, he had a vision that he wrote about in the book of Revelation. After an angel showed him wonderful things, John fell at his feet to worship him.

But he said to me, *"Do not do it! I am a fellow servant with you and with your brothers who hold to the testimony of Jesus. Worship God!"*

Revelation 19:10

13

ngels Are Majestic Beings

When I consider Your heavens, the work of Your fingers, the moon and the stars, which You have ordained, what is man that You are mindful of him? . . . For You have made him a little lower than the angels.

Psalm 8:3–5, NKJV

I look around and marvel at all the things men and women have invented and discovered and done! Then I look up at the sky and realize we have been put here, 93 million miles from the sun, our source of heat and light, so that life can exist on our planet. Incredible interweavings of air and water, fire and earth, enable us to build a better life. I notice how my own body parts function without my having to do a thing: my heart beats, lungs breathe, stomach digests, eyes see, ears hear. How complex! How wonderful!

The Bible says angels are even more wonderful beings, higher in order than human beings. Let's find out more about them.

14

[In creation] the morning stars sang together and all the angels shouted for joy.

Job 38:7

Angels Are Warriors

"Don't be afraid," the prophet answered. "Those who are with us are more than those who are with them."... Then the LORD opened the servant's eyes, and he looked and saw the hills full of horses and chariots of fire all around Elisha.

2 Kings 6:16–17

Elisha's servant had been terrified to see the Syrian army with horses and chariots surrounding the city. But his eyes were opened to see the mountain full of horses and chariots of fire. Angel warriors surrounded Elisha!

John's Revelation tells that long ago a war was waged in heaven. The archangel Michael and his angels fought against the angel of light who wanted to take God's place and be worshiped (Revelation 12:7–9). Some of his names are the devil, great dragon, old serpent, destroyer, tempter, accuser,

hater and
deceiver.
So the devil—Satan,
the beautiful angel of
light, Lucifer—was thrown to
earth along with the angels who had followed him. He
still tries to overcome those who love God. But I do
not need to be afraid because Jesus in me is greater
than all the devil's power.

The chariots of God are tens of thousands and thousands of
thousands.

Psalm 68:17

17

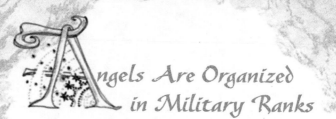

Angels Are Organized in Military Ranks

"Put your sword back in its place," Jesus said to him. . . . "Do you think I cannot call on my Father, and he will at once put at my disposal more than twelve legions of angels?"

Matthew 26:52–53

A legion was made up of six thousand disciplined, highly effective soldiers, along with several hundred cavalry troops. So when the Roman soldiers came to arrest Jesus, He had at least 72,000 powerful warrior angels at His command. But He chose to let the puny "cohort" (a division of a legion, probably six hundred soldiers) arrest Him.

The devil has his military organization, too. He, too, has legions. Once Jesus met a man who was so wild that he continually broke chains and cut himself. No one could control him. When he saw Jesus, he ran up and begged not to be tormented. When Jesus asked his name, the man replied, "Legion." Jesus made all those demons leave (Mark 5:1–20).

Imagine the power and organization
in the courts of heaven!

"A river of fire was flowing, coming out from before [the Ancient of Days]. Thousands upon thousands attended him; ten thousand times ten thousand stood before him. The court was seated. . . ."
Daniel 7:10

Angels Appear in Human Form

> *The LORD appeared to Abraham near the great trees of Mamre while he was sitting at the entrance to his tent in the heat of the day. Abraham looked up and saw three men standing nearby. When he saw them, he hurried . . . to meet them and bowed low to the ground.*
>
> *Genesis 18:1–2*

Abraham's visitors were angels — God visiting him in human form. After sharing a meal, they told Abraham that in one year he would have a son, even though both he and Sarah were too old to have children. And it happened just as the angels said.

Have you ever met a stranger you suspected might have been an angel? I have a friend, Hope McDonald, who wrote a book of stories people told her about strangers they thought were angels. Many people have had an experience with angels and have a story. Why not ask your friends and family to tell you theirs?

The writer of the letter to the Hebrews told the new Christians that a guest might be not a raggedy old man or woman but an angel:

*Do not forget to entertain strangers, for by so doing some
people have entertained angels without knowing it.*

Hebrews 13:2

ngels Protect and Punish

"What if there are fifty righteous people in the city? Will you really sweep it away and not spare the place for the sake of the fifty righteous people in it? . . . What if the number of the righteous is five less than fifty? . . . forty? . . . thirty? . . . twenty? . . . ten?" [God] answered, "For the sake of ten, I will not destroy it."

Genesis 18:24–32

Abraham's nephew Lot lived in Sodom, a city where people did many wicked things and only laughed at God. Abraham probably did not think he had much influence with God that day when he was visited by the angels, so his prayer was not very bold. Maybe he did not have the courage to ask God outright to save Lot and his family, who were only four people (not even ten). But God sent His angels anyway, because Lot loved God and Abraham had prayed for him.

Often the Bible mentions that angels travel in pairs and protect people, especially when others are praying. Have you ever thought that your prayers could help the angels protect someone? If you think

a problem is too small or too big to solve, take it to God and let Him decide!

When [Lot] hesitated, the [angels] grasped his hand and the hands of his wife and of his two daughters and led them safely out of the city, for the LORD was merciful to them.

Genesis 19:16

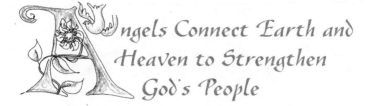

Angels Connect Earth and Heaven to Strengthen God's People

[Jacob] had a dream in which he saw a stairway resting on the earth, with its top reaching to heaven, and the angels of God were ascending and descending on it. There above it stood the LORD.

Genesis 28:12–13

Jacob was a young man running for his life from his brother, Esau, who wanted to kill him for cheating and stealing from him. One night under the stars with only a rock for a pillow, Jacob had a dream in which God promised to be with him and help him. He had been wrong to cheat and steal from his brother, but God still had a purpose for him. The angels helped him to see that.

Have you ever done something that makes you feel cut off from God?

Are you in a hard place right now? God still has a purpose for your life, just as He did for Jacob. The angels are still going up and down the ladder to maintain the connection between earth and heaven and help you be strong!

When Jacob awoke from his sleep, he thought, "Surely the LORD is in this place, and I was not aware of it. . . . How awesome is this place! This is none other than the house of God; this is the gate of heaven."

Genesis 28:16–17

ngels Do Miracles

The angel of the LORD appeared to [Moses] in flames of fire from within a bush. Moses saw that though the bush was on fire it did not burn up.
Exodus 3:2

When God wanted to get Moses' attention, he sent an angel. Moses' first response was curiosity. Then, when he realized a miracle was taking place, he took off his sandals and hid his face because he was afraid. But even though he felt unworthy, he accepted God's call.

All the rest of his life Moses walked and talked with God. He saw the terrible miracles of the ten plagues in Egypt and the wonderful miracle of the Red Sea opening so that three million Hebrews could cross over, escaping slavery. Angels helped the Israelites during forty years of wandering, protecting them with a cloud of fire to keep them warm at night and a cooling cloud to shield them from the scorching sun during the day.

God
wants to
get our atten-
tion, too. Have you
had an extraordinary
experience—something
that could not be explained? God is calling to you as
He was to Moses. Expect a miracle!

When we cried out to the LORD, he heard our cry and sent an angel and brought us out of Egypt.

Numbers 20:16

Angels Are Usually Invisible

Then the angel of the LORD moved on ahead and stood in a narrow place where there was no room to turn, either to the right or to the left.

Numbers 22:26

Balaam was a prophet tempted to use his gift from God in order to gain a profit! Though Balaam did not want to be stopped or corrected, God sent an invisible angel. Balaam's donkey was able see the angel with a sword in his hand and swerved to miss him twice, while Balaam whipped the animal. Then the angel moved so that there was nowhere the donkey could go. The donkey lay down and refused to budge, making Balaam even angrier—until God opened his eyes to see the angel, too.

How is God trying to correct me today? Am I like Balaam, wanting to go my own way, not knowing an angel stands there because I am going the wrong way?

Open my eyes, Lord, to see things as they really are, and send Your angel to lead me in Your way.

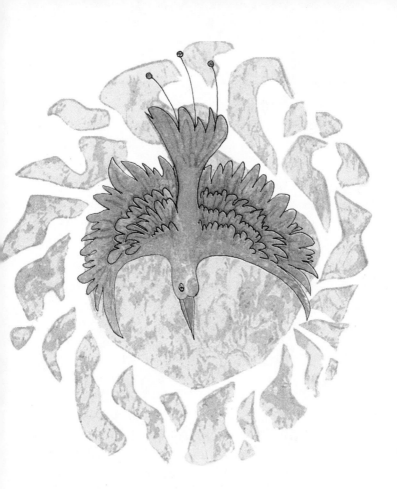

*Balaam said to the angel of the L*ORD, *"I have sinned. I did not realize you were standing in the road to oppose me. Now if you are displeased, I will go back."*

Numbers 22:34

29

Angels Are Powerful

When Joshua was near Jericho, he looked up and saw a man standing in front of him with a drawn sword in his hand. Joshua went up to him and asked, "Are you for us or for our enemies?" "Neither," he replied, "but as commander of the army of the LORD I have now come."

Joshua 5:13–14

After Moses' death, Joshua was told by God to lead the people into the Promised Land. Joshua had been a spy in the land. He knew how good and fruitful it was, but that those who lived there were fierce and big as giants. He also knew that his people were not strong enough by themselves to move into that land without being destroyed. Now Joshua, a strong man, stood in the presence of a powerful being and fell face-down to the ground. The angel told him to take off his sandals because that place was holy.

Even the greatest and most powerful of angels recognize God as their only and supreme authority. They cannot be on my side (as Joshua learned) if I

am not on God's side. In every problem too big for me, I can ask, "Am I on God's side?" If I am, then He may send an angel to help. Look at what one angel can do:

"Because you have prayed to me . . . I will defend this city and save it . . . !" Then the angel of the LORD went out and put to death a hundred and eighty-five thousand men in the Assyrian camp. When the people got up the next morning — there were all the dead bodies!

Isaiah 37:21, 35–36

ngels Are Chosen by God for Special Missions

When the angel of the LORD appeared to Gideon, he said, "The LORD is with you, mighty warrior."
Judges 6:12

To his family and friends and even to himself, Gideon was no mighty warrior. He was not brave enough to stand against the bullies who had persecuted the people of Israel and ruined their crops for seven years in a row. But in answer to Israel's prayer, God sent an angel to help Gideon drive away the enemy. Though at first Gideon was afraid and unwilling, he followed the Lord's instructions and the enemy fled.

Do you know God has chosen you for a special mission—maybe even a mission that to you seems impossible? Remember, there are mighty angels to help us carry out even what seems impossible!

Let [my ene-
mies] be like chaff
before the wind, and let the angel of the LORD chase them.
Let their way be dark and slippery, and let the angel of the
LORD pursue them.

Psalm 35:5–6, NKJV

Angels Stand by God's People in Danger

> "The God we serve is able to save us from [the blazing furnace], and he will rescue us from your hand, O king. But even if he does not . . . we will not serve your gods or worship the image of gold you have set up."
>
> Daniel 3:17–18

Shadrach, Meshach and Abednego were Jewish youths who loved God but lived in exile in Babylon. The Babylonian king, Nebuchadnezzar, was a proud man who ordered that everyone in his empire worship a golden image, or die. When the three youths refused to bow down, the king was furious and ordered them thrown into a huge fiery furnace. The fire was heated seven times hotter than usual, so that even the soldiers who tied them up were killed.

But the king was amazed to see the young men alive in the fiery furnace. And who was that fourth man walking unharmed in the fire? It was an angel of the Lord who rescued the three from danger. Seeing that, King Nebuchadnezzar worshiped God:

*Then Nebuchadnezzar said, "Praise be to the God of
Shadrach, Meshach and Abednego, who has sent his angel
and rescued his servants! They trusted in him. . . ."*

Daniel 3:28

# ngels Provide

Men ate the bread of angels. . . .
Psalm 78:25

Elijah had been through a terrible test and was worn out. He had challenged and killed 850 false prophets, whose god had done nothing, while Israel's God had answered with fire. Now the evil queen Jezebel was threatening to kill Elijah, so he ran for his life into the wilderness.

Why was Elijah afraid of the queen now? Hadn't his simple prayer brought down fire from heaven? But the Bible says he was so discouraged, exhausted and afraid that he wanted to die. When he awoke from a nap under a tree, an angel was touching him, saying, "Get up and eat." Under the tree he found a loaf of bread baked on hot stones and a jar of water. This happened twice. It gave him strength for forty days (1 Kings 19:1–8).

Even the strongest person has times of feeling weak and afraid. Tell someone you trust about a fear you have. Pray together that God will provide what you need. Maybe it will be through an angel, though you do not realize it!

The ravens brought [Elijah] bread and meat in the morning and bread and meat in the evening, and he drank from the brook.
1 Kings 17:6

Angels Guard

For he will command his angels concerning you to guard you in all your ways. . . . You will trample the great lion and the serpent.

Psalm 91:11, 13

Even though it was against King Darius' law, Daniel, a Hebrew exile who had risen to great power in the royal court, worshiped God, kneeling in prayer three times a day. King Darius admired Daniel for his wisdom and was upset to learn that Daniel had broken the law and was supposed to be thrown into the lions' den.

The next morning at dawn the king rushed to the pit and had the stone rolled away. "Daniel," he called, "has your God, whom you serve continually, been able to deliver you from the lions?" Daniel was unhurt, thanks to the angel God had sent who had "shut the mouths of the lions," and gave all praise to God (Daniel 6).

Are there any wrong laws that keep you from doing what you know God wants you to do? What about the law against prayer in public schools? Should you pray anyway? Does prayer have to be aloud and in public? If God sent an angel to help you if you were unjustly punished, in what ways might the angel help?

"See, I am sending an angel ahead of you to guard you along the way and to bring you to the place I have prepared."

Exodus 23:20

39

ngels Are Wise

*The angel who was speaking to me left, and another angel
... said to him: "Run, tell that young man, 'Jerusalem
will be a city without walls. . . . And I myself will be a
wall of fire around it,' declares the Lord, 'and I will be its
glory within.'"*

Zechariah 2:3–5

When the prophet Zechariah was just a young man, God gave him wisdom through angels. They told him things he could not know about his nation's future. Zechariah trusted the angels' information because it matched the wisdom from God given through other prophets throughout Israel's history. Angels know only what God tells them.

Wisdom from God gives blessing and understanding. It instructs, keeps from evil, preserves life, makes strong, is better than gold or jewels and produces good fruit (James 3:17). Jesus is our wisdom (1 Corinthians 1:30).

Whom do you consider wise? Have you ever said or done something wise? Why do you think so?

40

My dear friends, don't believe everything you hear. Carefully weigh and examine what people tell you. Not everyone who talks about God comes from God.

1 John 4:1, TM

ngels
Are God's Messengers

An angel of the Lord appeared to him, standing at the
right side of the altar of incense. When Zechariah saw
him, he was startled and was gripped with fear.
But the angel said to him: "Do not be afraid,
Zechariah; your prayer has been heard."
Luke 1:11–13

Another Zechariah (500 years
after the prophet Zechariah) was
in the Holy of Holies, per-
forming the duties of
priest in Jerusalem, when
something extraordinary
happened. An angel came
to bring him a message from God.
Zechariah was so unbelieving that
the angel told him he would not be able to
speak until the message — that God would
give him and his wife a son — came true.

42

If an angel brings a message from God, it is God's will and it will come true. Can you think of other messages an angel brought? What about the Christmas story? the Easter story? If God were sending you a message today, what do you think it might be? Messages from God teach, strengthen, encourage, comfort, convict of sin, bring forgiveness.

The angel answered, "I am Gabriel. I stand in the presence of God, and I have been sent to speak to you and to tell you this good news."

Luke 1:19

43

Angels Obey God's Will

Praise the LORD, you his angels, you mighty ones who do his bidding, who obey his word. Praise the LORD, all his heavenly hosts, you his servants who do his will.

Psalm 103:20–21

Gabriel was busy following orders. He was the angel chosen by God to go to Zechariah as he served in the Temple in Jerusalem to announce that his wife, Elizabeth, would give birth to a son, John the Baptist. Then God sent Gabriel to the little town of Nazareth to give an important message to a young woman named Mary. She would have a baby named Jesus; He would be a great King, the Son of the Most High God.

Has God ever told you to do something specific?

The Bible has many commandments that help us to live pleasing to God. All are general commandments for everyone, but some are specific to individuals. Do you love God enough to do what He says?

[Jesus Christ] has gone into heaven and is at God's right hand—with angels, authorities and powers in submission to him.

1 Peter 3:22

Angels Announce Salvation

An angel of the Lord appeared to him in a dream and said, "Joseph . . . you are to give him the name Jesus, because he will save his people from their sins."

Matthew 1:20–21

Joseph was in a tough situation. The lovely young girl he was engaged to marry was now expecting a baby. This was a crime punishable by stoning to death for the Jewish people. Then the angel explained in a dream that Mary had not sinned. God's Spirit had done this in order to save His people. Joseph understood that the angel's message matched the messages of the prophets who spoke for God throughout the history of his people. A Savior would come and be born of a young woman, like Mary. So Joseph did what the angel of the Lord had said.

Have you ever had an angel dream? Did it match with the message of the Bible? It helps me to write my dreams in a notebook, pray about them and, if they match with the Bible, do what they direct. The angels want you to find your part in God's plan and help you do it.

You . . . have now heard for yourselves — through the Holy Spirit — the Message of those prophecies fulfilled. Do you realize how fortunate you are? Angels would have given anything to be in on this!

1 Peter 1:12, TM

Angels Sing Praises to God

Suddenly a great company of the heavenly host appeared with the angel, praising God and saying, "Glory to God. . . ."

Luke 2:13–14

Imagine being on that dark hillside near Bethlehem with the shepherds! The stars sparkled like diamonds in a black velvet sky, but one star shone especially bright. Then the quiet was broken by the song of heavenly beings. Whatever the language, the shepherds understood that the glorious creatures of light were singing praises to God.

If the angels, so close to God, who know Him better than I, delight in adoring, thanking, praising God in song, I, too, can draw closer by filling my heart with praises. It is fun to ask Him for a new song, to sing those thoughts and melodies that rise up from the deep, quiet place within me.

What
is your
new song?

*I heard a sound from heaven like the roar of rushing waters
and like a loud peal of thunder. The sound I heard was like that
of harpists playing their harps. And they sang a new song. . . .*
Revelation 14:2–3

Angels Warn

An angel of the Lord appeared to Joseph in a dream. "Get up," he said, "take the child and his mother and escape to Egypt. Stay there until I tell you, for Herod is going to search for the child to kill him."

Matthew 2:13

God sends angels to warn us of dangers that some-times cannot be seen with earthly eyes. God knew Herod's heart. As puppet king of the Jews during Roman rule, Herod had to scramble for power, prestige and wealth. Herod was desperately afraid that someone else would be as ruthless as he to take over his throne.

Joseph obeyed the angel's warning about Herod and took his family to Egypt, returning only when the angel appeared again in a dream to tell that the danger was past.

Have you ever felt guided around or through some danger? Have you ever had a dream that seemed a clear message from God? What happened? Did you disobey the warning, like Jonah, or find safety by obeying it, like Joseph?

*An
angel
of the Lord
appeared in a dream to
Joseph in Egypt and said, "Get up, take
the child and his mother and go to the land of Israel,
for those who were trying to take the child's life are dead."*
Matthew 2:19–20

Angels Help in Healing

There is in Jerusalem . . . a pool . . . [where] lay a great multitude of sick people, blind, lame, paralyzed, waiting for the moving of the water. For an angel went down at a certain time into the pool and stirred up the water.

John 5:2–4, NKJV

By that pool was a man who had lain there 38 years, unable to get into the water when the angel came because he had no one to help him. How lonely and discouraged he must have been, to know help was so close and yet have no hope of being healed! But God knew all about his hurt and frustration, his longing to be made whole, and sent Jesus that Sabbath day to heal him.

Is there a problem or sickness in your life that only God can cure? Jesus still asks, "Do you want to be well?" And do you know that *you* can be an angel for someone else who is hurting? God can touch and heal others through you.

A little later Jesus found him in the Temple and said, "You look wonderful! You're well! Don't return to a sinning life or something worse might happen."

John 5:14, TM

Angels Comfort

Jesus said to him, "Away from me, Satan! ..." Then the devil left him, and angels came and attended him.

Matthew 4:10–11

Jesus began His mission after God sent His Spirit on Him at His baptism and said, "You are My beloved Son in whom I am well pleased." After that wonderful acceptance, Jesus faced forty days in the desert alone without food. Satan tempted Jesus to change God's plan and meet His own needs for food, popularity and power. Jesus said no each time, but it was not easy, because Satan knows just what temptations are hardest for each of us to overcome. After Jesus' struggle, angels came to bring comfort to Him. We do not know *how* they ministered. Was it with food and drink, a big hug or a sense of God's presence like healing light shining through all the hurt places?

How have you struggled with temptation? Have you ever sensed some "extra" help ministering comfort to you?

*Are not all angels ministering spir-
its sent to serve those who will inherit
salvation?*

Hebrews 1:14

Angels Are Joyful

There is rejoicing in the presence of the angels of God over one sinner who repents.

Luke 15:10

Jesus told about a lost sheep rescued by the good shepherd (Luke 15:3–7) and about a son who wasted all his inheritance, was sorry and was welcomed home by his father with much rejoicing (Luke 15:11–32). Jesus told about a woman who lost one of her treasured silver coins. She swept and searched until it was found. Then she was so happy she called her friends and neighbors in for a party (Luke 15:8–10).

The angels know and are sad when I wander away from God's perfect plan. When I am "found," they celebrate with God, just like the friends of the woman who found the coin.

The angels are not joyful all the time because they are participating with the whole creation that groans and suffers the pain of childbirth (Romans 8:22). But when one of those children comes forth, realizing God's wonderful love, they rejoice and have a party!

You have come to . . . the city of the living God. You have come to thousands upon thousands of angels in joyful assembly.
Hebrews 12:22

ngels Strengthen

*An angel from heaven appeared to him and strengthened him.
And being in anguish, he prayed more earnestly, and his sweat
was like drops of blood.*

Luke 22:43–44

Jesus came to Jerusalem where He knew that, though He was popular at the moment, the people would soon turn against Him. He knew a terrible death awaited Him. He came to the Garden to pray with His closest friends nearby, but they did not understand His suffering and fell asleep. Just then an angel came to strengthen Him. God did not change the plan that meant death to His only Son, but He gave Jesus the strength to endure.

Have you ever felt at the end of your strength? What helped you to endure? One night I felt I could not face another day and asked my husband to pray for me. I heard and felt the brush of angel wings around my head and was strengthened.

*. . . He became their Savior. In all their distress he too was
distressed, and the angel of his presence saved them. In his
love and mercy he redeemed them; he lifted them up and carried them all the days of old.*

Isaiah 63:8–9

Angels Are Radiant

In speaking of the angels [God] says, "He makes his angels winds, his servants flames of fire."

Hebrews 1:7

When the women went to Jesus' tomb on Easter morning, they were startled by an angel sitting on the stone. So bright was the angel that he looked "like lightning, and his clothes were white as snow" (Matthew 28:3). Though the angel looked like a man, the dazzling light around him let those who saw him know that he was a supernatural being. The guards were frozen with fear. At first the women were terrified, too, and bowed to the ground, covering their faces (Luke 24:5). God's holiness and the women's realization of their unworthiness made them afraid. But the angel told the women not to fear.

Have you ever experienced God's presence as light? Have you ever felt afraid of God? Why?

I looked up and there before me was a man dressed in linen, with a belt of the finest gold around his waist. His body was like chrysolite [a clear gem], his face like lightning, his eyes like flaming torches, his arms and legs like the gleam of burnished bronze, and his voice like the sound of a multitude. . . . I had no strength left, my face turned deathly pale and I was helpless.

Daniel 10:5–6, 8

ngels Proclaim Jesus' Resurrection

The angel said to the women, "Do not be afraid, for I know that you are looking for Jesus, who was crucified. He is not here; he has risen, just as he said. . . . Go quickly and tell his disciples: 'He has risen from the dead. . . .'"

Matthew 28:5–7

After the women received the message from the angels, they were still afraid but filled with joy. They hurried to tell the others the good news about Jesus, their resurrected Messiah.

What does the resurrection of Jesus mean to you? Have you encountered the risen Jesus? Have you, like the women, told others about Him?

The angels, those brilliant beings, consider it a privilege to proclaim the resurrection of Jesus, whom they continuously worship and adore.

And I looked, and I heard the voice of many angels around the throne . . . saying with a loud voice, "Worthy is the Lamb that was slain to receive power and riches and wisdom and might and honor and glory and blessing."

Revelation 5:11–12, NASB

ngels Ask Penetrating Questions

Mary [of Magdala] stood outside the tomb crying. As she wept, she . . . saw two angels in white, seated where Jesus' body had been, one at the head and the other at the foot. They asked her, "Woman, why are you crying?" "They have taken my Lord away," she said, "and I don't know where they have put him."

John 20:11–13

At her answer, Jesus appeared behind her and asked her the same question.

Is He also asking me why I cry, to help me see the true reason for my sorrow and grief? Am I lonely, afraid, unable to trust God without someone with me I can depend on for help?

Mary learned that Jesus is alive, though in a different way than before. My world that seems so real is not the only reality. The supernatural world of the angels and the resurrected Jesus is as close as my tears.

"Death has been swallowed up in victory." "Where, O death, is your . . . sting?" . . . Therefore, my dear brothers, stand firm. Let nothing move you. Always give yourselves fully to the work of the Lord, because you know that your labor in the Lord is not in vain.

1 Corinthians 15:54–55, 58

Angels Bring Judgment

Herod . . . delivered a public address to the people. They shouted, "This is the voice of a god, not of a man." Immediately, because Herod did not give praise to God, an angel of the Lord struck him down, and he was eaten by worms and died.

Acts 12:21–23

Herod, the king responsible for killing John the Baptist and James the brother of John, wanted to be like the Roman emperors who said they were gods. He did not, like Peter (Acts 10:26), silence those who adored him. So an angel silenced Herod.

When the Bible describes the future, it mentions angels who punish, bringing God's judgment and order to the world. God has the power to judge fairly because He knows all things.

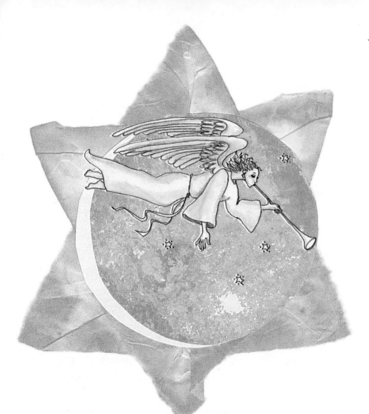

He gives me power to forgive and have mercy on those who wrong me. Is there someone who makes me really angry whom I need to forgive today, even if he or she is wrong and I am right? Can I do something today to correct some injustice?

The Lord Jesus shall be revealed from heaven with His mighty angels in flaming fire, dealing out retribution. . . .
2 Thessalonians 1:7–8, NASB

Angels Carry Believers to God in Death

"The beggar died and the angels carried him to Abraham's side."
Luke 16:22

The experience of death comes to every living creature. Because "the valley of the shadow of death" is unknown, most people fear it. But the angels took the beggar, Lazarus, to a good place. After Jesus was raised from the dead, angels took Him into heaven. He conquered everything that is to be feared about death, so we can trust that angels will come for us, too. They will take us to the place Jesus has prepared for us when it is His time.

Do you know anyone who has died? Perhaps you have heard about someone who has died and come back to life. My husband says that one night when his heart stopped beating, bright and loving angels helped him through a dark tunnel where all that was "chaff" in his life burned away, leaving only that kernel that was God's will. What does God want me to do now? That is the important question.

Archangel thunder! God's trumpet blast! . . . [We] will be caught up with them into the clouds to meet the Master. Oh, we'll be walking on air! . . .

　　　　　　　　　　　　1 Thessalonians 4:16–17, TM

Angels Bring Peace

A hand touched me and set me trembling on my hands and knees. . . . Again the one who looked like a man touched me and gave me strength. "Do not be afraid, O man highly esteemed,"he said. "Peace!"

Daniel 10:10, 18–19

Daniel lived to old age as a foreigner faithful to the living God in the courts of unbelieving kings. Once when he had been praying for three weeks, an angel appeared, touched him and told him his prayer had been heard 21 days before. An invisible battle had been fought in the heavens, the angel told him, and "the prince of the Persian kingdom" had been resisting him. Then Michael, the archangel, "one of the chief princes," had come to help Daniel's angel.

Peace of mind and peace in the family, neighborhood, nation and world do not come easily.

Angels
join us in
the struggle
against forces of evil that try to prevent peace.

What areas in your life need peace? Ask God what your part is to help bring about healing, wholeness and peace in the world. Ask God to send an angel to help.

I urge . . . that requests, prayers, intercession and thanksgiving be made for everyone—for kings and all those in authority, that we may live peaceful and quiet lives in all godliness and holiness.

1 Timothy 2:1–2

ngels Stand with Jesus' Followers

They were looking intently up into the sky as he was going, when suddenly two men dressed in white stood beside them.

Acts 1:10

It was Jerusalem after the Passover feast. The disciples had many memories of traveling there each year, but this year was unique. The Rabbi had broken bread and said it was His body broken for them. The Passover wine, He said, represented His blood. Then He had been arrested, tortured, crucified. But amazingly the chains of death had been broken; He appeared to them many times in the following forty days. Now, when He left them, they were not alone. These "two men dressed in white" were standing beside

them again. The angels had been in the Garden, then in the tomb, and were encouraging them now not to just stand there. So they returned to Jerusalem to do what Jesus had said—wait for God's Holy Spirit.

Do you know what Jesus wants *you* to do as you wait for His Second Coming? Have you asked for God's Holy Spirit to come in your life? He is the One "who stands beside."

"You will receive power when the Holy Spirit comes on you; and you will be my witnesses."

Acts 1:8

73

Angels Deliver

During the night an angel of the Lord opened the doors of the jail and brought them out. "Go, stand in the temple courts," he said, "and tell the people the full message of this new life."

Acts 5:19–20

Peter had seen angels at work; they had told him, "Jesus is risen!" After the Holy Spirit came with tongues of fire, Peter enjoyed an awareness of God's holy closeness that he had not known even as he walked with Jesus every day. Then the trouble started. It was dangerous with church and state to tell what he had seen and heard about Jesus, and Peter and the other apostles were thrown into jail.

But an angel of the Lord opened the gates of the prison and delivered them.

After James was killed by King Herod (Acts 12:2), Peter was thrown into prison again, this time with two guards chained to him. But an angel came in the middle of the night, a bright light shone, his chains fell off and the prison gate opened (Acts 12:1–19).

Why do you think Peter and the apostles were set free? Have you ever felt you were set free — delivered from something that kept you bound? Do angels set us free every time we are in trouble? In what other ways can we be set free?

The angel of the LORD encamps around those who fear him, and he delivers them.

Psalm 34:7

ngels Direct the Activities of God's People

An angel of the Lord said to Philip, "Go south to the road—the desert road—that goes down from Jerusalem to Gaza." So he . . . met an Ethiopian eunuch. . . .

Acts 8:26–27

In order for Philip to be at the right place at the right time to meet the right-hand man of the queen of Ethiopia, God sent an angel to direct him. Philip had the answers to the man's questions. He explained how Jesus is the One spoken about throughout the Old Testament Scriptures, as Jesus had told His followers on the Emmaus road. The lesson was fresh, the sense of timing urgent. The Ethiopian was baptized right there in the stream by the road and went back to his country with the good news that Jesus is the Messiah!

Have you shared your faith with someone you did not know because it seemed just the right time and place? What if Philip had been too shy to speak to the Ethiopian, or said his faith was too private to share?

When they came up out of the water, the Spirit of the Lord suddenly took Philip away, and the eunuch did not see him again, but went on his way rejoicing.

Acts 8:39

Angels Witness

"Cornelius, a centurion, a righteous and God-fearing man well spoken of by the entire nation of the Jews, was divinely directed by a holy angel to send for you."

Acts 10:22, NASB

Peter would have rejected the three messengers from Cornelius, a Roman, had he not received a dream-message from God telling him that God had sent them. It was hard for Peter to overcome his feelings of superiority, and for Cornelius to believe that he could be accepted by the community of Jesus' Jewish followers. So God sent an angel. The Holy Spirit came on everyone with such wonderful expressions of praise pouring forth—in their common languages and in that of the angels—that they knew God was welcoming Cornelius and his friends and relatives into the family of believers.

Have you ever had to overcome some stubborn prejudice or pride? What helped you to overcome it?

Who in God's family is hard for you to accept? Why? Would praising God and seeing that person from His perspective help?

"I now realize how true it is that God does not show favoritism."

Acts 10:34

Angels Encourage

"I urge you to keep up your courage, because not one of you will be lost; only the ship will be destroyed. Last night an angel of the God whose I am and whom I serve stood beside me and said, 'Do not be afraid, Paul. You must stand trial before Caesar; and God has graciously given you the lives of all who sail with you.'"

Acts 27:22–24

Paul was a prisoner on a ship headed for Rome. Luke wrote an eyewitness account of the dangers of that journey. After a storm raged for several days, they had to throw their supplies overboard. Days later the storm had still not subsided and the crew of the ship (who had stopped eating) thought they were going to die. Then the angel came to encourage Paul so he could encourage his shipmates.

Being a Christian is not easy. There are difficulties to be faced. But God finds ways to encourage us and enable us to keep standing firm through whatever rough

times we face. Paul's angel appeared to him in person to help him keep up his courage. What has helped you make it through a difficult time in life? Can you encourage someone else in turn?

"Be strong and courageous. Do not be terrified; do not be discouraged, for the LORD your God will be with you wherever you go."

Joshua 1:9

Angels Are Holy

"When he finally arrives, blazing in beauty and all his angels with him, the Son of Man will take his place on his glorious throne. Then all the nations will be arranged before him and he will sort the people out."
Matthew 25:31–32, TM

The holiness of Jesus and His angels is a down-to-earth sort, including concern for the hungry, thirsty, ragged and homeless poor. This holiness reaches out with help and healing to the sick, with kindness and liberating compassion to those locked in various kinds of prisons. Jesus has called us to this kind of servant/friend holiness because His plan for us goes beyond the earth. After everything is wrapped up, we are to judge the world and the angels, too (1 Corinthians 6:2–3). Imagine!

Other words for *holiness* are *righteousness, justice* and *love.* Is there someone you could call holy? What makes you think so?

*"If any of you
are embarrassed over me . . .
when you get around your fickle and unfocused friends, know
that you'll be an even greater embarrassment to the Son of
Man when he arrives in all the splendor of God, his Father,
with an army of the holy angels."*

Mark 8:38, TM

Angels Are Harvesters

Another angel came out of the temple and called in a loud voice to him who was sitting on the cloud, "Take your sickle and reap, because the . . . harvest of the earth is ripe."

Revelation 14:15

The book of Revelation is filled with angels and awesome acts—thunder, lightning, the earth reeling under cosmic justice. The images of a holy God and His heavenly harvesters startle and strike fear. As C. S. Lewis wrote about Aslan, the Lion, "No, he is not safe." Our God, who is often described in terms of warm fuzzies, has a dark side that can be described only with apocalyptic imagery. Even those most intimate with God can at best cry, "Lord, have mercy."

What do you think the crop is that the angels will harvest from the earth?

Jesus' parables dealt with the earth yielding crops of thirty, sixty and one hundred percent. He spoke of our being grafted into Him, the Vine, pruned and producing good fruit that others can enjoy.

The angel swung his sickle on the earth, gathered its grapes and threw them into the great winepress of God's wrath.

Revelation 14:19

Angels Reveal What Is Real

One of the seven angels . . . said to me, "Come, I will show you the bride, the wife of the Lamb." And he . . . showed me the Holy City, Jerusalem, coming down out of heaven from God.
Revelation 21:9–10

Often I am caught up in the ordinary struggles of daily life and cannot see the grand plan of God throughout the ages. Scripture points to times in the lives of those eager for God's perspective when angels revealed spiritual realities truer than what can be seen with our eyes. The bride of Jesus is the Church. Often I see only the divisions, the superior attitudes, the complicated separation of groups. Angels showed John the Church in a new light, bathed with God's glory, a vehicle for God's mercy with healing streams to be poured out on all who will come. Angels urged

John to worship Jesus, to expect His soon coming, to live in the expectant urgency of the ordinary bathed in His glory.

"I, Jesus, have sent my angel to give you this testimony for the churches. I am the Root and the Offspring of David, and the bright Morning Star. . . . Yes, I am coming soon."

Revelation 22:16, 20

ngels Are Guardians

> *"Whoever humbles himself like this child is the greatest in the kingdom of heaven. And whoever welcomes a little child like this in my name welcomes me. . . . See that you do not look down on one of these little ones. For I tell you that their angels in heaven always see the face of my Father in heaven."*
>
> *Matthew 18:4–5, 10*

You and I have guardian angels; Jesus said so! The filthiest beggar in the street has a guardian angel. The meanest man and grouchiest woman have guardian angels, too. That just reminds me that I have personal contact with God all the time, and so does every other person, even though I may not like him or her.

Your guardian angel is with you to do all the things angels do: guard, guide, protect, instruct, reveal God's will, praise Him always!

For I am convinced that neither death nor life, neither angels nor demons, neither the present nor the future, nor any powers, neither height nor depth, nor anything else in all creation, will be able to separate us from the love of God that is in Christ Jesus our Lord.

Romans 8:38–39

Angel Stories

This page is for you to write your own angel story. You might also want to write angel stories your friends have told you about that you want to remember. Always ask yourself if the angel was sent by God. If from God, the angel will always honor the name of Jesus (1 John 4:1–3).

Then I looked and heard the voice of many angels, numbering thousands upon thousands, and ten thousand times ten thousand. They encircled the throne and the living creatures and the elders. In a loud voice they sang: "Worthy is the Lamb, who was slain, to receive power and wealth and wisdom and strength and honor and glory and praise!"

Revelation 5:11–12